The Javaad Alipoor Company

T0353202

THINGS HIDDEN SINCE THE FOUNDATION OF THE WORLD

written by **Javaad Alipoor** with **Chris Thorpe**

Co-commissioned by HOME
and The National Theatre of Parramatta

THINGS HIDDEN
SINCE THE FOUNDATION
OF THE WORLD

Written by **Javaad Alipoor** with **Chris Thorpe**
Co-created by **Natalie Diddams** and **Javaad Alipoor**
Dramaturg **Chris Thorpe**
Directed by **Javaad Alipoor**
Performed by **Javaad Alipoor** and **Asha Reid** with
Raam Emami, together with onstage musician **Me-Lee Hay**

Set, costume and lighting design by **Ben Brockman**
Composer and musician **Me-Lee Hay**
With music by **Raam Emami**
Sound design by **Simon McCorry**
Projection and video design by **Limbic Cinema**
Additional Filming by **Tate Creations**
Production Management **The Production Family**,
Dom Baker and **Tom Mackey**

Company Stage Manager **Dylan Tate**
Technical Stage Manager **Rebecca Lee**
Production Assistant **Freya Hastings**

The Javaad Alipoor Company takes stories beyond the stage through powerful multi-platform creations that explore the intersection of politics and technology in the contemporary world. Established in 2017, it stands on the shoulders of Northern Lines, the first company founded by Javaad Alipoor – a British-Iranian, Manchester-based and Bradford-built artist and writer – and retains its commitment to making new work with diverse artists for diverse audiences and communities. In 2017, Javaad began writing a trilogy of plays about how technology, resentment and fracturing identities are changing the world. *The Believers Are But Brothers* (2017) used a live WhatsApp group and theatre to explore masculinity, violence and the internet. The play toured the world and in 2018 the company was commissioned to adapt it into a film for BBC4. The play's sequel – *Rich Kids: A History of Shopping Malls in Tehran* (2019) – used an Instagram feed and live show to explore the growing gap between the rich and the poor, climate change and the way we imagine ourselves. When Covid-19 paused touring, *Rich Kids* was adapted into an original digital experience which played at online festivals in 2020, including Sundance Film Festival and Under the Radar festival.

In 2020 the company delivered two digital projects: *What is a Muslim*, a collaboration with graphic artist and calligrapher Razwan Ul-Haq, exploring contemporary Muslim identity, and *The Colour of Our Politics*, created with actor and broadcaster Tanya Vital, a podcast series about how the UK has been shaped by a rich history of anti-racist activism and resistance. In 2021 Javaad collaborated with Chris Thorpe to create *Made of Mannheim*, a new trilingual theatre production inspired by Schiller's *Jungfrau von Orleans* exploring identity, religion and linguistic diversity. The full show was produced with and presented by Nationaltheater Mannheim and Theaterhaus G7. We also began the development of *Pop Icons*, a musical heritage project celebrating culture and music with migrant communities across England.

Javaad Alipoor
Writer, director and performer

When I started researching the story of Fereydoun Farrokhzad, I came to realise that his murder is the beginning of a series of events that still haunt us today. As the relationship between the Global North and the Global South has shifted, so too has the old sense of the West as a safe place where dissidents can escape to. Put simply, you might leave the dictatorship, but the dictatorship won't leave you.

Things Hidden Since the Foundation of the World is the final part of a trilogy of plays that I began writing in 2017. I knew I wanted this last part to stand alone whilst speaking to the relationship between politics and technology, history and the present that has been the thread connecting all three plays. Retelling and trying to understand how to retell this story has helped me find a way to do that and to really confront what it means to think of the world as something like the internet, research as a kind of deep dive and tracing the way the 'democratisation' of the thirst for knowledge reproduces older networks of power.

A lot of research went into making this show, if you would like to learn more, we have put together a list of some good places to start:

Iran's Long Reach? How Dissident Showman Fereydoun Farrokhzad Was Murdered Far From Home. A Documentary by Radio Free Europe

Iran Between Two Revolutions by Ervand Abrahamian

Can the Subaltern Speak? An essay by Gayatri Chakravorty Spivak

A Subaltern Studies Reader, 1985–1995 by Ranajit Guha

BIOGRAPHIES

Javaad Alipoor | Writer, Director, Performer
Javaad Alipoor is a British-Iranian, Manchester-based and Bradford-built artist, writer, performer and Artistic Director of The Javaad Alipoor Company. He wrote, directed and performed in *The Believers Are But Brothers* for the stage and for BBC Four; *Rich Kids: A History of Shopping Malls in Tehran*, co-created with Kirsty Housley, for the stage and for its digital world tour which included a run at the prestigious Sundance Film Festival; and together with Chris Thorpe he wrote and directed the trilingual theatre production, *Made of Mannheim*, which had its world premiere at Nationaltheater Mannheim and Theaterhaus G7. Javaad was Resident Associate Director at Sheffield Theatres from 2017 to 2018 where he directed Dale Wasserman's 1963 play, *One Flew Over the Cuckoo's Nest*. Prior to this he was Associate Director at Bradford's Theatre in the Mill from 2015 to 2017.

Chris Thorpe | Writer, Dramaturg
Chris Thorpe is a writer and performer from Manchester. His work tours and is produced in the UK and internationally. He has collaborated with Javaad on several projects, including dramaturgy on *The Believers Are But Brothers* and *Rich Kids: A History of Shopping Malls in Tehran*, as well as co-writing and dramaturgy on *Things Hidden Since the Foundation of the World*. In 2021 Chris and Javaad also co-wrote and directed *Made of Mannheim* for Nationaltheater Mannheim, Germany. Chris also has ongoing collaborations with artists and companies including Rachel Chavkin, China Plate, Yusra Warsama and Portugal's mala voadora. Work as a writer includes *Victory Condition*, and the film *What Do You Want Me to Say* for the Royal Court, *There Has Possibly Been an Incident* and *The Mysteries* for the Royal Exchange and *Beowulf* for the Unicorn. Upcoming work includes *The Soprano Always Dies*, for mala voadora/Portuguese National Opera, *Always Maybe The Last Time* for the Royal Court, and *A Family Business* for Staatstheater Mainz/China Plate.

Natalie Diddams | Co-Creator
Natalie Diddams is a dramaturg, director and academic researcher based in Manchester. Notable productions include *A Series of Metaphors About a Plague* (Home Manchester); *The Believers Are But Brothers* (international tour); *B!RTH* (Royal Exchange Theatre); and *Thesmo* (national tour). Natalie has a PhD from Manchester Metropolitan University, and is a full-time Teaching Fellow at the University of Warwick. Through her research, Natalie is a leading voice on the intersection between comedy and contemporary politics, and regularly hosts workshops and performances aimed at empowering participants through comedy. Natalie is an Associate Artist of The Javaad Alipoor Company, Trestle Theatre, and the International Schools Theatre Association (ISTA). More information can be found at www.nataliediddams.com and she is @DrDiddamsComedy on Instagram.

Asha Reid | Performer

Theatre includes: *One Jewish Boy* (Trafalgar Studios); *Snowflakes, One Jewish Boy* (Old Red Lion); *Pufferfish* (Vault Festival); *Graceful* (RADA Studio/Rosemary Branch); *Inside Pussy Riot* (Les Enfants Terribles); *Biggest Tarantino Fan in the World* (Vault Festival/Arcola); *Edinburgh Test* (Pleasance/Old Red Lion); *Stay Happy Keep Smiling* (Jermyn Street); *I Found Joy in a Hopeless Place* (Hackney Showrooms); *Money Womb, Hacked* (Theatre503); *A Third* (Finborough); *Scarlet* (Southwark Playhouse); *Electra* (Old Vic); *Cross Purpose* (Crypt Gallery); *Medea* (The London Theatre); *The Hate Play* (Box Clever); *Miniaturists: The Interval* (Arcola); *Scarlet* (Bush); *The Tempest* (Watford Palace); *Lord of the Flies* (Broadway Theatre); *The Magpies The Wolves* (Tristan Bates/Pleasance); *The Beggar's Opera* (Regent's Park Open Air).

Film includes: *FEMME* Feature Film, *FEMME* Short Film (BIFA Winner & BAFTA Nominated); *Horror Vacui, Into Me See, Face The Camera and Smile, House Hold, Gemma's Wedding, Puzzled, White Collar, Weird Love.*

Television: *The Syndicate* (BBC1); *Nutritiously Nicola* (London Live).

Raam Emami | Performer

Raam Emami is an Iranian/Canadian musician. He started his musical career as the founding singer/songwriter of Hypernova, a post-punk band which was born in the undergrounds of Tehran in the early 2000s, before pursuing a solo career under the pseudonym, King Raam. Raam is the son of the prominent professor and environmentalist, Kavous Seyed Emami, who was arrested in 2018 on false charges of espionage and imprisoned in Iran's notorious Evin Prison, where he later died in suspicious circumstances. Since then, Raam has lived in political exile in Canada where he uses music and advocacy to bring global attention to those persecuted by the regime. His taboo-smashing podcast, *Masty o Rasty (The Drunken Truth)* has been streamed more than 20 million times.

Me-Lee Hay | Composer and Musician

Me-Lee Hay composes for film, TV, dance and theatre. A Malaysian born Chinese-Australian, she has had works shown across many platforms including Netflix, Australian commercial TV channels and mainstream cinemas plus international platforms such as UKTV, planetariums and international film festivals including Cannes and Sitges. Off the screen, Me-Lee has been commissioned by leading arts companies of Australia such as Sydney Dance Company's PPY and Sydney Theatre Company for *White Pearl* (which toured nationally). She has also performed and composed for *Yellow Yellow Sometimes Blue* (The Joan, Penrith) and composed and sound designed for *Guards at the Taj* and *Launch Pad* (National Theatre of Parramatta). Classically trained in piano and cello, Me-Lee is a graduate of the Australian Film Television & Radio School (AFTRS), is an Associate Composer Representative of the Australian Music Centre and the Vice President of the Australian Guild of Screen Composers. She is published by Gaga Music.

Ben Brockman | Set, Costume and Lighting Design

Benjamin Brockman is an Australian award-winning lighting and set designer.

A few career highlights are as follows: *Family Values, Splinter, Replay, Diving for Pearls* (Griffin Theatre Company); *Things Hidden Since the Foundation of the World, Lady Tabouli, Girl in the Machine, The Girl/The Woman, The Sorry Mum Project, Let Me Know When You Get Home* (National Theatre of Paramatta); *Overflow, Torch Song Trilogy, Broken, Detroit, The Mother Fucker with the Hat, Tinderbox* (Darlinghurst Theatre Company); *Carmen Alive or Dead, Razorhurst* (Hayes Theatre Company); *Horses, Jess and Joe Forever, Greater Sunrise* (Belvoir 25a); *Tribes, The Big Dry, The Plant, Neville's Island* (Ensemble Theatre); *Farnace* (Pinchgut Opera); *Are We There Yet?, Guess How Much I Love You, Spot Live On Stage* (CDP); *Sissy Ball 2022, Sissy Ball 2020* (Sydney Mardi Gras Festival); *Mirage* (Campbelltown Arts Centre); *Cleansed, Metamorphoses, Angels in America Part 1 and 2* (Redline Productions); *Coram Boy, Dresden, Visiting Hours, The Laden Table, Jatinga* (bAKEHOUSE); *The Day of the Triffids* development, *Good Omens The Musical* development, *Herringbone, Grey Gardens, Man of La Mancha* (Squabbalogic); *Symphonie Fantastique* (Little Eggs Collective); *In The Zone, King* (Shaun Parker & Company); A full portfolio of work can be found at www.benbrockman.com

Simon McCorry | Sound Design

'Blissful, serene and yet broken at the edges to reveal something unseen' *Magazine Sixty.* 'The leading voice of McCorry's cello is an irresistible beam of light in the darkness' *The Quietus* '…electro-orchestral drone-scapes of, by turns, gauzy intimacy and soaring grandeur' *Mojo*

Simon McCorry was born in London of mixed Indian/British ethnicity, studied music at The Centre for Young Musicians & Morley College, philosophy at Durham University and is now based in Stroud, Gloucestershire. Has worked as a composer and sound designer in theatre, film and contemporary dance for over 20 years. Recent work is a combination of loop-based cello compositions and atmospheric improvisations, field recordings and modular synth. linktr.ee/simonmccorry

Limbic Cinema | Projection and Video Design

Limbic Cinema is an award-winning multimedia creative studio that specialises in projection mapping and immersive video design. The studio creates mesmerising, meaningful and memorable encounters that empower people through the use of light, sound and moving images. Directing and collaborating on ambitious productions that utilise cutting edge tools and immersive technology to transform spaces and transport audiences. Animation is central to the studio's output, taking traditional workflows and expanding on them through the use of emerging technologies. Their work can be seen in theatres and music halls, at festivals, large-scale public events and online. Recent work featured at Video Mapping Festival, Lille (*Spectra*, 2022), Glastonbury Festival (*Temple*, 2022), Edinburgh Fringe (*Megalith*, 2022), Sundance Film Festival (*Rich Kids*, 2021), Vivid Sydney (*Critical Point*, 2021). Limbic was nominated by CreaTech (Creative Industries Council) as one of the 'Ones to Watch' in 2021.

Dylan Tate | Company Stage Manager

Dylan Tate has worked in a range of roles across the industry since 2008. He splits his career as a stage manager, director and videographer, often producing and consulting on work across the UK with companies and individuals. He has toured internationally and around the UK as a filmmaker and performer. A founding member of Flabbergast Theatre, Associate Artist of Futures Theatre Company and Director of Tate Creations. Enjoying all aspects of theatre and film, he is proud to be involved with The Javaad Alipoor company.

Rebecca Lee | Technical Stage Manager

Rebecca Lee recently returned home to England and is delighted to be working with The Javaad Alipoor Company. She has spent the last 15 years working in Singapore and South East Asia as a Theatre Educator and Production Manager. Management credits include: *Asian Youth Theatre Festival* (Philippines: 2021, Myanmar: 2020, Malaysia: 2019, Singapore: 2017–2018), *Under the 5 Trees* (National Gallery Singapore, 2019); *National Language Class* (National Gallery Singapore, 2016/17); *Play Me I'm Yours* (Luke Jerram, Singapore 2016); *Singapore River Festival* (2015). A strong believer in the promotion of accessible arts education, Rebecca also ran Buds Youth Theatre (Singapore) from 2008 to 2022.

With thanks to: **Caroline McCormack, Joanne Kee, Daniel Holdsworth, Kirsty Housley, Tanuja Amurisya**, and **Portland Institute of Contemporary Art**.

HOME

Head to HOME to discover new art, new experiences and new stories, from our city and across the world. Everyone is welcome. HOME work with international and UK artists to produce entertaining, extraordinary experiences, creating an exciting mix of thought-provoking film, art, drama, dance, and festivals, with a strong focus on new commissions, and talent development. HOME's ambition is to push the boundaries of form and technology, to experiment, have fun, take risks and share great new art with the widest possible audience.

NATIONAL THEATRE OF PARRAMATTA

Riverside's National Theatre of Parramatta (NTofP) is making bold, transformative and inspirational theatre nurturing creative communities and speaking to a new wave of global theatre-making. We are committed to presenting and fostering authentic, inclusive voices and welcoming new audiences. NTofP creates, commissions, presents and tours performances that resonate with and reflect contemporary Australia's place in the world. Believing in the power of theatre, NTofP also nurtures talent through its engagement and skills development opportunities with programs that provide access, visibility and infrastructure for our vibrant local community now and into the future.

THINGS HIDDEN SINCE THE FOUNDATION OF THE WORLD

Javaad Alipoor with Chris Thorpe

Characters

JAVAAD/NARRATOR
ASHA/PODCASTER
RAAM/MUSICIAN

Note on Performance

In the original production, the text was divided between three
performers. Javaad Alipoor, who as co-writer/director spoke in
direct address, presenting his research to the audience and
illustrating this with projection. Asha Reid played the podcaster.
Her text was delivered from a live podcasting booth, hidden
behind projection screens. Raam Emami played himself,
emerging from a musician's recording studio, also hidden
behind projection screens. Through the course of the play
Raam's scenes move from virtual to real, being projected the
first time we see him, then broadcast live, and his final two
scenes given in direct address

*This text went to press before the end of rehearsals and so may
differ slightly from the play as performed.*

Scene One

JAVAAD/NARRATOR. Over the past couple of years I've
written two shows. The first was called *The Believers Are
But Brothers*, and it was about young men who join ISIS or
the alt-right, and the second was called *Rich Kids: A History
of Shopping Malls in Tehran* and it was about the obnoxious
lifestyles of the kids of the Iranian super-elite.

Both these stories are about people I have a gap from. In the
case of the first show, about ISIS and the alt-right, that gap's
pretty obvious. I've got Muslim heritage, but I'm a bit too
rum-and-Coke adjacent for anyone in ISIS to give me the
time of day. I had even less luck wandering into 4chan. And
in the second show, about the children of the Iranian elite –
I'm a bit less the kind of Iranian you find cruising round
Tehran in a Lamborghini, on loads of coke, more the kind
you find taking cheap speed in the passenger seat of a Ford
Escort in West Yorkshire.

Each show starts with a world we don't understand some key
things about. And it's my job to make myself a bridge over
that void, that gap, for the audience.

Part of building that bridge was talking about the tools –
WhatsApp, Instagram – the people in them use to
communicate with each other. But when I was thinking about
this show, I realised there's a more fundamental set of tools –
some technological and some just ways of thinking – that
I was using to get my hands on the basic facts about these
people. Not the tools the people in the story use, but the tools
I use to make the story. Tools we all use, reflexively, to fill in
the knowledge gaps in the world when we find them.

In principle, we think every gap in our knowledge can be
filled. And the everyday tools we use to do that shape me,
and you and this. So I'm going to tell you a story I already

know, but one which has a gap at the centre of it for everyone, no matter if you know it or not. And then we're not so much going to do a deep-dive, we're going to think about why the idea of a deep-dive makes us believe we understand the world better.

The story I already know is the story of Fereydoun Farrokhzad. He was an Iranian pop star. Iconic and easily recognisable to Iranians. Like the Iranian Tom Jones. After the revolution in '79, when Khomeini ousted the Shah, Fereydoun Farrokhzad went into exile. He lived as a refugee in Germany.

His life is well documented apart from the last four or five days – all we know about that period of his life is he spent a proportion of it dead. In August 1992 his body was discovered in his small flat in Germany, when his neighbours alerted the police that his dogs had been barking for two nights. The German police never solved the case. To put it simply, imagine there was an Iranian Tom Jones but he was for some reason forced into exile, then found mysteriously and brutally killed.

For me and other Iranians, the story of his murder is the void – the gap in the middle, in the sense that it is unsolved. To non-Iranians, that void is contained within a bigger void. There are more things you need to know. Who he was, for a start. What his songs meant to people. What the factions of Iranian politics were. What it's like to live as a refugee from the Global South in the Global North. And of course we expect me to fill that void with a story. Maybe even use the bit of my identity I share with some of the people in that story to represent them in some way.

Let's start with my relationship to this story, then. Which from one angle is about an Iranian refugee. Now I'm not an Iranian refugee, but my dad is, and my mum's a white English woman. I'm also, as it happens, artistic director of a theatre company and I'm standing here talking to you. So for those of you in the audience who have never been refugees, or indeed Iranian, but are just here to see a show, I have an important role – you'll trust me to represent two worlds – and I can translate those worlds to each other. I stand in a position where I can say a thing in one world is *like* a thing in another and you'll believe me. We're all used to certain ways of doing that translation when we sit in a theatre.

One of the most common, for example, is using an artefact of diasporic popular culture, usually brought by a parent or grandparent, from wherever home was, to explain something about that culture, and the culture it was taken to, and the position of the speaker as someone existing in a new space *their* existence has created in the new culture.

If the artefact that crossed cultures was a Fereydoun Farrokhzad record then that show might start like this:

I stand here and look at you, not as a single human figure, but as the interplay of two vast tides of history. One which flows from the East India Company's colonial hunger through the discovery of oil in what became Iran, through British and Russian occupation to American airbases, the rule of the Shah, and the SAVAK secret police. To a young Islamist revolutionary, fleeing the Shah on the first plane he could board. The other tide, the one that built the great industrial cities of northern Europe – in this case, *the* great city of northern Europe, Bradford. To its cold and drizzling streets, the unending hunger for labour, its cosmopolitan pockets where foreigners were welcome. Two tides of history, intertwining the destiny of that Iranian man with that of a young white woman. And from those destinies, a child.

This is a show about who we are and how we come to be who we are. The ocean-passing airplanes, the accidents that make us. It's about diaspora and imperialism and war.

It's about Iran. It's about the West. But most fundamentally, it's about me.

I come from a hybrid background. I'm mixed race and mixed culture. I speak English like my mother and Persian like my *baba*. When I speak, I speak for a history you tried to squash and ancestors you tried to silence, but I also speak for you.

I grew up in the same northern England as my white friends, amongst the same rotting factories. Those friends went home to the smell of white bread, but for me home smelled of this, yes, but also olives and saffron.

Once, playing cricket, I misjudged when I jumped to catch a ball, and my hands met another of my white friend's hands. His fingers were stained with tomato ketchup, where mine were purple with pomegranate juice.

When my father came to this country, he brought a handful of tapes. Recordings made of the sound of the country he thought he would never see again. He and my mother would put music on from their youth, so in the car on the way to an auntie's house or on the front-room stereo we would listen to two worlds' worth of music. Abba. Bob Dylan. Joan Baez. Yes, but sometimes those tapes that came from the East in a tattered suitcase so many years ago. Sometimes Fereydoun Farrokhzad.

The world carries the scars of colonialism and imperialism and war. And racism. And in the next ninety minutes we can heal them. Because art is a kind of medicine made from dream and memory. *It* can heal them. I think if I can understand how the world brought me to this moment, remembering those tapes in that car – then we will truly understand each other. And if we truly understand each other, I can tell you what we need to overcome that history – and we can do it together.

I'd probably then start banging on about decolonising the marketing of hummus or something.

But that isn't the play we're doing.

Scene Two

JAVAAD/NARRATOR uses an iPad connected to an electronic whiteboard to make notes and illustrate.

JAVAAD/NARRATOR. There are three ways I as a writer have to do my research if I want to tell a story about why Fereydoun Farrokhzad was killed.

Obviously, the first one is the internet.

Human societies tend to assume that the deepest part of human consciousness is a bit like whatever tool is dominating society at that time. Freud talks about pressures and pneumatic metaphors of the psyche; Marx talks about the steam engine of human history at exactly the same point as the industrial revolution. There's probably a parallel ancient-history version of this show where a Sumerian version of me is explaining how we often think of our minds as a giant bit of clay full of accounting tablets. It's no surprise that we think of our mental tools as similar to whatever's in our hands. Which in our case isn't steam engines, but information.

At the heart of information technology is data science. Data is, strictly speaking, the opposite of noise. And noise is whatever isn't data.

There is no better internet research tool, for sorting the data from the noise, than Wikipedia. It's become the place we all go to do that.

One of the great pleasures of lockdown for me was falling into Wikipedia rabbit holes. I spent the first and most stringent period reading almost everything that English Wikipedia has about Jainism, the Indian religion. Many happy days later, still having not met a Jain or read a book about their religion, I don't actually have that clear an idea about what Jains think or do. But I'll still tell you all about them at parties.

In any case, falling into a Wikipedia rabbit hole can tell you something really interesting about how the information we have easiest access to is structured. So, if you grab your phones – I want someone to call out for me something, anything, that we can all look up on Wikipedia.

Audience member calls something out.

Okay. If we all go to that page, just for the next thirty seconds or so – click on anything you think looks like an interesting link. And then from that page, click on the next link that looks interesting, and so on.

Okay. Who ended up where?

Audience members call out the pages they have landed on. JAVAAD/NARRATOR *notes them on the iPad.*

Great. Just keep those pages open on your phones for now. So obviously there's a show in which I explain the murder of Iran's most celebrated pop star and its relationship to post-colonial politics, by improvising a story using [*X/Y/Z*], in the style of popular nineties panel show *Whose Line Is It Anyway?*

But we're not doing that – because there's something even weirder going on on Wikipedia. Start from whatever page you ended up at. Click on the first non-definitional hyperlink you come to. A non-definitional hyperlink is the first blue text which isn't in brackets. Do the same thing on the next page, and the next, and the next… In something like ninety-six per cent of cases, you will end up in a loop between articles about human experiences, or feelings, and articles about logic, or facts. Where Wikipedia looks like a diffuse network of ideas connecting to each other, it's actually organised quite rigidly – bouncing between the abstraction of truth, and the solidity of facts as if they're interchangeable. And nobody really knows why.

That way of trying to understand leads us into a kind of delusion that the world is knowable, with enough effort, because it's already known. The kind of delusion that leads me to talk about Jainism at parties or stand in supermarkets looking at 'Persian Style' hummus, thinking – it is vital the Western misconception that hummus is somehow Iranian is corrected by repeated unnecessary references to it in my next show.

After internet research, the next tool I have is constructing stories. In Farrokhzad's case, I have the story of his life, which ends in his unsolved murder. In a show, you need to choose the form for your story – and the obvious form for this story is a murder-mystery podcast. Because it seems like they constitute about eighty per cent of human culture these days – and because, well, it's the story of a murder. So I worked with a theatre-maker and podcaster called Asha Reid, and asked her to try and put together a murder-mystery-style podcast about Fereydoun Farrokhzad – specifically about the competing theories around why he was killed. We'll hear some of it throughout the show. We'll hear it in Asha's voice. Speaking to us in the way podcasts speak to us.

ASHA/PODCASTER (*from her booth*). The voice that speaks straight into your ear with quiet authority. The voice that sounds like this. Hi.

Scene Three

JAVAAD/NARRATOR *puts the iPad down. He reveals a projection screen.*

JAVAAD/NARRATOR. So we've got the tools that help us find things. We've got the tool of the story we make from what we find out. And the third tool I have at my disposal is political theory.

Political theory is what you use to connect history and the present in a way that feels more useful.

And to do that, in this show, we are going to use the theory of subalternity.

There is a pretty good Wikipedia entry on this, so please, go ahead. I'll put some music on. Have a read through, maybe have a look at some of the references. I'll give you about twenty minutes.

Beat.

Just kidding, you can turn your phones off now. Long story short – the idea is that colonial and post-colonial power dynamics set up a certain relationship between cultures.

A *subaltern* culture is one that exists either outside, or in the gaps of, a dominant culture. And to the dominant culture, it's invisible. Subaltern groups don't write history. They were the natives in colonised society. They're the masses in a post-colonial state. And in a very different way, they're refugees in rich countries. Because of this, members of the dominant group can live their whole lives without thinking about the subaltern groups, whereas the subaltern groups have to think about the dominant groups all the time. Fereydoun Farrokhzad is invisible to everyone apart from, mostly, Iranians, because nobody apart from them ever has to think about him.

Which is why, thirteen and a half minutes ago, I told you that Fereydoun Farrokhzad was a bit like the Iranian Tom Jones.

When I say Fereydoun Farrokhzad is like the Iranian Tom Jones, I'm pointing out that most of the world is made up of the kinds of places where, no matter how famous you get, you still have to be the 'someone else' of your country. And that 'someone else' has to come from the kind of place in which Tom Jones just stupidly exists and doesn't have to be explained.

Do we have anyone here with heritage in the Global South?

JAVAAD *takes a volunteer.*

Who is the [X]-ian Tom Jones?

But of course, translation is not a perfect way of representing. Fereydoun Farrokhzad isn't the Iranian Tom Jones. Aside from anything else, Tom Jones is the Iranian Tom Jones, insofar as people were buying his records in Iran, in the seventies. More importantly, Farrokhzad was different in loads of important ways. As well as being a sex symbol and a pop star, he was one of Iran's most important TV producers. He supported the careers of loads of musicians who went on to become stars themselves. He had a PhD in political science. What's more, his art and his personality got him chased from his country, and ultimately put his life in danger. As far as I'm aware, Tom Jones spent a lot of his life abroad, but he didn't end up in Vegas because he was fleeing the Great Welsh Islamic Revolution.

So there are a lot more things to say than: he was the Iranian Tom Jones. To have any idea what happened in his story, it's not enough to just translate the showman in him. He was also someone who had to give up stardom and start again as a refugee. He was a musician and artist, who ended up much more political than he ever sought to be. He was also someone who ended up in a country not too different to this one, but with his life in a danger he couldn't escape.

Wouldn't it be outrageously convenient and structurally useful, if somewhere on my travels I had met a singer who shares those specific aspects of Farrokhzad's story? Who could be a modern representation. Of the journey he made. Of the way a regime has tried to repress him. Someone whose arguably best-known song was used for a political purpose that he never particularly envisaged. And to cap it all off spoke English and, happened to be, you guessed it, Iranian.

Well, luckily for us. I did. When I was researching this show, I met a contemporary Iranian rock star called Raam. Iranians will probably know him from his recording name, King Raam. Parts of his story will help to fill in some of those gaps.

Scene Four

RAAM/MUSICIAN (*on the video played on the projection screen*). There's two things you need to know about me. The first is how I got here.

The geographic timeline of my life goes like this – I was born in Iran, went to the States when I was two years old, back to Iran between ages ten and seventeen, when I went to Canada. Back to Iran again when I was twenty, returned to the US when I was twenty-six. When I was thirty-four, Rouhani, the reformist, came to power and I returned to Iran. I left for Canada a few years later for reasons I'll get to. I live in Vancouver. Or more accurately that's where what little stuff I own is.

I became a singer by accident, because in Iran, at the age of twenty, I joined a band in the underground punk scene. As in, you generally had to play a venue so far underground the police couldn't find it, because when they inevitably did, you got the shit beaten out of you.

I'd got used to having the shit beaten out of me the first time I lived in Iran. A teacher once punched me in the head because I asked why the Prophet would have had an opinion on me listening to my walkman. I wasn't disrespecting the Prophet, and it wasn't about the walkman, really. I was just wondering aloud why things are the way they are.

But what you need to know is that I'm American, Canadian and Iranian. I have a passport for the last two of those. But Iran has forced me to be Iranian. Not in a bureaucratic sense. I just have no choice but to engage with that part of myself. The extra irony being, they'd rather I didn't.

My dad was a secular humanist, a conservationist, and a sociologist. He worked at one of the most right-wing, religious universities in the country on principle, because he believed the future elites should be taught by at least one guy who would contradict the party line – keep the door open to other worldviews at least a tiny amount. He believed in that, and the survival of the endangered Asiatic Cheetah, and the benefits of good weed. I was a deadbeat singer who didn't believe in much. Now I'm a famous singer, with a podcast in Persian about believing in things that's listened to by millions of people, and my dad's dead. Those two things are linked. We'll get to that later. But that's who I am, and how I got here.

Oh, and the second thing you need to understand, although you probably do already – outside of the Persian-speaking world, nobody knows who the fuck I am.

I used to work in a pretty upscale kebab restaurant in Toronto – yes, white British people, it is possible to have an upscale kebab restaurant. They did pomegranate-infused martinis. And the young Iranian-Canadian part of the clientele would freak out when they recognised me. There would be selfies, which I hated, and joy, which I liked. And the non-Iranians who just liked upscale kebabs would be fucking confused, and ask me a version of the question that's in some of your heads now. Which boils down to – are you what these other people think you are, or are you just some guy? Well the answer is: yeah. I'm both.

Scene Five

JAVAAD/NARRATOR (*as if in the process of writing the show*). It's late and there are four documents open on a laptop screen, three notebooks on the desk. Scattered paper. I'm trying to string together my thoughts and notes into something worth saying in public. I know I've done this before, but I don't feel like there is a coherent me I can access who has managed it – just a series of different people I used to be who somehow got this process right by accident. So I silence that worry. That feeling of being lost. I silence it by naming facts. Whether they're the most useful ones at this point is secondary to my need for them. If I can string them together to bridge the yawning space between the idea I start with and the one I want to land on, I can avoid looking at it too deeply.

It's not what it should be. Which means I'm not what I should be. I feel myself start to fail. I start to chip away at what's good about it, until I fuck it up again. Maybe I didn't know enough to start. Maybe that's it. I click another link, and another tab opens.

Scene Six

ASHA/PODCASTER. Welcome to *Death in the Gaps*. A podcast that wants to shine a light on mysterious unsolved murders, revealing the truth behind the way the world works, and the invisible and deadly stories we don't even notice on our own bloodstained doorsteps.

I'm going to get in close and say this, right into your headphones. Welcome. You're sitting in your kitchen. Maybe you're in the bath. Perhaps you're on the bus to work. Jogging. You've managed to squeeze a little extra moment for some more content. And you've chosen a kind of content that speaks to the world you live in. You are utilising your spare attention. You are gaining understanding. You are becoming a better global citizen through research. Good for you.

Let me start by saying thanks – and, here's the traditional, seemingly unrelated story at the start of the podcast to intrigue you, and also to casually give me the authority that comes from having a slightly cooler life than yours.

A few years ago, I was living in Portland, Oregon. I ended up being sort of taken in by an older Iranian couple who took pity on me. I was studying full-time, as well as working at a vegan doughnut shop, and they would drop off the occasional stew and whatnot. Anyway, they invited me to their daughter's wedding, and there was one particular song everyone really went off for. 'Asheyaneh', by Fereydoun Farrokhzad.

They ended up telling me this was pretty far from traditional Iranian wedding music – but that it reminded them of old Iran, in this super-iconic way. And they told me about how he had gone into exile but carried on making music, and how the singer, Fereydoun Farrokhzad, was, ultimately, horrifically killed.

This is a series about the mysterious murder of Fereydoun Farrokhzad. It's a mystery that is full of competing theories, and each episode we'll get into one of them. But before we do that, we need to state the facts of the case.

To do that, I'm going to switch into the present tense. It's a classic podcast tense-shift. You change the quality of your attention. Now I've got you. Let's go.

It's early August, 1992. In Bonn, West Germany, the police are breaking into a small apartment above a shop. There are dogs barking inside, which is why the neighbours have called them in the first place. The barking gets louder and more painful on the ears as the door is broken down, although the noise quickly becomes the least of their concerns.

The first noticeable thing is the heat of an oven left on for two days, and then the smell. The living room of the small apartment is spread for an Iranian meal. A floorcloth strewn with upended nougat and pistachio bowls. The body lies across the cloth, which has forty-eight hours of blood and gore soaked into it. It's a man. Barely recognisable. Knife used like a hammer. Rough holes punched into face and neck. The heat from the open oven door has melted parts of the corpse. Skin burnt. Human fat and blood congealed in a layer under the kitchen cabinets.

Maybe a robbery. They think. But the only things missing from his apartment turn out to be a personal planner and a relatively cheap Canon camera. Hardly a huge haul for this level of violence.

He's an Iranian refugee. That much the police can possibly guess. It's harder to tell from the modest apartment that he's also a political dissident, and incredibly famous in his native country. The German police never solve the case.

My sources are Wikipedia, as ever, and a few English-language websites with translations of articles about the murder which, let's face it, is deep enough. You might be chopping a carrot now, or unable to sleep. Whatever you're doing, there's a gap, a not-quite-enoughness of stimulation, and you can convince yourself I've done the work to fill it. If you're watching on YouTube, I'll cut some screengrabs of the articles into the video, and if you're listening to the podcast – I'll put links in the show notes. You won't click on them, but you'll feel better equipped to understand the world just knowing they're there.

In any murder investigation, the first port of call is those known best by the victim. A friend or a lover. The vast majority of murders are committed by someone the victim knew already. And the vast number of podcasts start looking at the most obvious theory first. So, conveniently for me, this is the line of inquiry the German police follow.

A number of witnesses had reported Farrokhzad meeting two men at the train station on the last day he was seen. He was well known in the Iranian community for welcoming new refugees into his home. But the police quickly dismiss this, seeming certain that Farrokhzad was killed by one person. Only two places were set for dinner. Two bowls of traditional Iranian nougat and fruit were spilled across the floor.

The Iranian government, never slow to capitalise on the death of an opponent, unofficially spread a rumour, suggesting that the murder was committed by a male lover; a twenty-seven-year-old Iranian immigrant who was also living in Germany. In the context of the intensely macho and homophobic culture of Iran, this could be seen as an attempt to discredit a legacy, and damp down public mourning for a critic. Or to look at it in a more cynical way: draw attention away from who actually committed a crime.

But even used cynically, this possibility wasn't pure invention, Fereydoun Farrokhzad had been dogged by rumours about his sexuality for many years. Even at the height of his fame in Iran.

In fact, near the end of his life, Farrokhzad himself had come close to coming out. In a video from his own personal archive, he can be seen openly discussing the issue of his sexuality. He says: 'I have this bravery, this courage, so I will stand in front of you like a man and I will tell you what I think. For four years of my life, I lived with a man, and I loved him to bits.' So the lover-as-suspect theory, even though it plays into prejudice, can't be dismissed as pure invention.

And so one of the first lines of inquiry concerned that. In progressive Europe, the prevailing homophobia of the time meant even minds presumably as open as those of the West German police go first to a pick-up, or a love affair gone wrong.

The Iranian immigrant and alleged lover was never named.

Is the bath water a bit too cool? Maybe think about running the hot tap for thirty seconds.

An SFX crash and the podcasting studio disappears.

Scene Seven

RAAM/MUSICIAN *is speaking from a pre-recorded, semi-transparent projection. Behind this, the real* RAAM/ MUSICIAN *plays music in a studio.*

RAAM/MUSICIAN. The punk band I started in Iran end up in the USA. And we become a media sensation, of a kind. In the eyes of MTV we were supposed to represent like the downtrodden youth of Iran who were fighting back. So we were a story. Because the countries of the Axis of Evil aren't also supposed to contain Joy Division fans. That was the story. Which luckily for us eclipsed the music. And then we broke up.

I went from semi-successful minor media sensation as a semi-competent punk musician to just another guy couch-surfing in Los Angeles. I was a long way from anywhere I'd ever called home, missing Iran, and my parents. It was a low point. It was stasis, and failure, and drug-induced directionlessness all at once.

So when I fell in love, it felt like I'd been saved. And of course when I fell in love, I fell in love hard. I was desperate, which in certain lights can be mistaken for sexy, and she – her name was Tara – was caught up in the romance, being a poet, and we moved in after about forty-eight hours. Are we still together? What the fuck do you think? But for a while, for both of us, it was fucking beautiful. And I wrote some of the best songs of my life. We collaborated on the music and the lyrics, because how else are you going to fill the time when you're living with a poet? And for the first time in my life, at her insistence, I sang in Persian.

And nobody gave a fuck. Which was interesting. When I was in a mediocre punk band, singing in English, the Iranians thought I was subversive, and the Americans thought I was exotic. Now I was singing in Persian, the Iranians thought I was trying to be exotic, which they didn't love, and everyone else thought I was incomprehensible, so they ignored me. By this stage though I didn't care. But I threw it onto the internet for the small number of people who still did. The song I was most proud of was called 'The Hunter'. It was based on a poem Tara wrote. About the fact that in our pursuit of each other we are both the hunter and the hunted, and it sounded haunting, and lovelorn, and yeah we were disgustingly in love, but the song just worked.

This was around 2009. And part of the reason I wanted to be in Iran, I guess, was the Green Movement. Ahmadinejad had just straight up stolen an election, and people were finally sick of his shit. So they were out on the streets. And Ahmadinejad, being Ahmadinejad, met new challenges with old solutions, and shot them.

I couldn't do anything. I was a singer. A former punk singer with no political platform. But I wanted to be there.

And suddenly I was. There's a guy in Iran – look I know this show is partly about the weirdness of saying one thing is like another, but the quickest way to say it is he's like the Iranian Jon Stewart. He's called Kambiz Hosseini.

And when Kambiz Hosseini wants to pay tribute on his show to Neda Agha-Soltan, Mohammad Mokhtari, Saneh Jaleh, Sohrab Aarabi and the rest of the protesters who died in those Green Movement protests in 2009, who have become the face of democratic martyrdom, he cuts slow-mo footage of the protest, and them, to my song. To 'The Hunter'. Because for whatever reason it fits. One is not about the other, but they're both true, and their truths work together.

And my life fucking explodes.

Scene Eight

JAVAAD/NARRATOR. I can't tell you how big Fereydoun Farrokhzad was in Iran in the early 1970s. Basically he was a music star, yes. But also the host, 'showman' in Persian, of the very first big Friday-night show on Iranian TV. Of course, when I say Friday night, think Thursday night – because in the Muslim world you get Friday rather than Saturday off. But you call Thursday night, Friday night, because in Persian the night is called for the day that comes after it. His show was a phenomenon, suddenly there as if it had always been there, but unlike anything else before.

He was such a big deal that he launched dozens of careers. This is him on one of the episodes of his show, introducing the now legendary Shohreh:

Projected footage from YouTube, showing Fereydoun Farrokhzad singing with Shohreh –
youtube.com/watch?v=Qxibb_cOqTY.

If he was the Iranian Tom Jones, then his show was the Iranian… what? *Morecambe and Wise*? Mixed with the Thursday version of *Saturday Night Live*? In some ways, yes.

In that it was a cultural phenomenon shared by a huge segment of the population. But again the comparison falls apart. Saying his show was merely popular erases just what the sudden appearance of it in Iranian living rooms was like.

You don't necessarily know this, watching as a family in Iran in 1971, but you're living in a country that has some of the most advanced TV technology in Asia. In countries like Iran, development worked in a different way to Europe – there was national penetration of colour TV, before there were really even national newspapers.

So to try and describe the feeling of being the grandparents, parents, grandkids, watching this broadcast, live, necessitates being aware of what arrives in the room with the light. In a provincial town, in a small house with one main room, there is a large square floor. Sometimes a woven carpet is thrown across it, and it's a sort of dining room. Other times, sleeping mats and sheets and duvets. Now three generations sit around, leaning, cross-legged against cushions propped against the walls.

So Iran is modernising, in its own, inconsistent way, and this colour TV is part of that. But right now, in this room, and the family it contains, there are still older thoughts, about men and women and land, that maybe haven't changed so much. This show is those two realities trying to talk to each other. And you love it.

The music is of course familiar. It reminds you of an older kind of music. For the older people in the family, songs you would have heard sung, when you were young.

His dance moves would seem new, weirdly wooden. Not very manly. Men dance more forcefully at weddings and parties. This is more European. Her style is more fluid and more recognisable. But this kind of behaviour, a man and a woman so close together and dancing in this way, would feel very different if it wasn't on TV. But on TV it's fun. As long as it is on the TV, you can accept that this is your country, but it isn't your world.

Inside you, there are aspirations. Children to be married, more grandkids. You want one of them to finish school and study at university. You want your eldest son home safe from working in Tehran. There are the material things you want too. New fabrics to make clothes for new year. But there is no connection between these personal hopes and dreams and the way you feel towards what you're watching. It's a different world.

It's at least a fourteen-hour bus ride to Tehran. And then, if you went uptown to where these people live, you know you'd be the only person in a hijab. You are suddenly aware of seeing yourself through the eyes of the TV performers. The world you live and breathe and want in, wraps around theirs. It rearranges itself around the shards of light the programme produces. It, and you, are a mute background, they are on broadcast.

You're dimly aware there are other more famous singers, known beyond their countries in a way he isn't. But that doesn't matter right now, because in this country you're working out how to be part of, he is the world and he speaks to everyone. And he does it beautifully. He's louche. He's fun. He's playful. He holds women's hands and dances and jokes in front of everyone. The children like him. That's not really any way for a man to be, but for *this* man, you'll allow it.

For you, he isn't the Iranian Tom Jones. He is incomparable. He is the brightest star, albeit in a smaller sky.

You might be my grandmother, or any of the millions of other people in rooms like that. The decisions you made were the main driver of how your country changed. But even so. You can only exist in this room, now, insofar as I'm describing you.

And you only think of Farrokhzad as a brighter star in a smaller sky, because I make you. You wouldn't have thought of your culture, and global culture as skies of different dimensions.

You exist here because you're being mediated by this guy, who we've given the authority to do that, partly because of his link to you. But the real you is invisible and silent.

Scene Nine

ASHA/PODCASTER. Welcome to *Death in the Gaps*. A podcast that wants to shine a light on mysterious unsolved murders, revealing the truth behind the way the world works, and the invisible and deadly stories we don't even notice on our own bloodstained doorsteps. All directly into your ears whilst you take the train home from work, or dice an onion for dinner.

This series, we're looking at the mysterious murder of Fereydoun Farrokhzad. It's a mystery that is full of competing theories, and each episode, we'll get into one of them. This is episode two, so you're starting to get familiar with his name. Stick with it. Pronunciation is half the battle.

It's weird, isn't it? That he was a huge star? You zone out for a second. You look out of your windscreen or your living-room window. There's someone delivering an Amazon package. Maybe they're a famous painter from a country you don't think of often enough.

Last episode we talked about the theory that Farrokhzad was killed by a lover or a close friend and explained why that crime-of-passion narrative doesn't fit what we know. The German police did actually arrest one of Farrokhzad's friends, the man who was possibly his partner, and found he'd been in a different city altogether.

So what do we know? He was brutally killed while preparing a meal for two people. The only items taken were his Canon camera, which he used to take pictures of his many guests, and his personal planner.

One other thing you need to know about Farrokhzad is that he was not on good terms with the Iranian government. Not only had he fled, but he had a much more secular nationalistic view of Iran, which led him to see Islam as the problem with Iran that held it back as a country. A view not shared by Iran's famously Islamic government. So in the 1980s, in exile, he spent his time doing two things:

Sometimes, making happier videos, to cheer up refugees and keep them connected to their memories:

Projected footage from YouTube –
youtube.com/watch?v=opnOxQItiQk

But he also became more and more political:

Projected footage from YouTube –
youtube.com/watch?v=L-4J-SJj0bY

This video is from one of two sold-out concerts he gave at the Royal Albert Hall, less than a year before his death. He did a lot more than just sing the hits. He's gunning for the Iranian government.

You can't remember for a second the exact reason the government was so bad. But the main thing your mind sticks on is that the Albert Hall holds six thousand people so there must be at least twelve thousand people who feel sufficiently passionate about someone you've never heard of to fill it. That feels weird. But it's good to be reminded those people exist.

At the Albert Hall shows, his jokes about the new rulers of Iran get more and more on the nose. He jokes about their prudishness. Their fatwas around sex. And if that's not bad enough, he is saying that the British caused the Iranian revolution, and actually they are behind Khomeini. In front of thousands of Iranian emigres and exiles who probably want to believe conspiracy theories like that, even if they don't believe them already.

But, even given that criticism, is it really possible the Iranian government would have him killed? He's a singer. He's like Tom Jones.

Well, there had been a whole series of summary executions in Iran in the years after the revolution. Members of the elite, or of the SAVAK, the Shah's security apparatus, who couldn't get out in time. And then a kind of low-level civil war where the victorious party got rid of anyone who agreed the Shah had to go, but were too Maoist, or not religious enough, or the wrong sort of religious. Or anyone who got in the way, really. You get the picture. Then the Iran–Iraq War happened, and there was a further crackdown on dissent.

That said, by the time Fereydoun Farrokhzad was killed, all the other dissident groups had been squashed – and the war with Iraq was won – so why would they do it? I guess when you find something you're good at, it's pretty hard to stop.

There are of course ways Farrokhzad's killing doesn't fit the Iranian government's MO. The primary one is that, unlike most of their targets, Farrokhzad wasn't shot. The second is that he was killed much later, after the civil war and war against Iraq had been won, and his brand of dissidence had ceased to be as much of a threat.

But then, there are a mysterious set of killings of Iranian dissidents that mostly happened inside, but also outside the country from the late eighties to the late nineties – known in Iran as the chain killings.

The chain killings were a series of murders with similar MOs to that of Farrokhzad's death. In each case, a famous cultural or political leader was killed with brutal violence, usually stabbed or set on fire in their own home.

More than seventeen people were killed this way.

However, there is a problem with this theory. As part of the chain murders, the nationalist writers Daryoush and Parvaneh Forouhar were killed at their Tehran home. There was a public outcry. In the public perception, things had gone too far and someone needed to take the blame. Three secret policemen were arrested and admitted to the crimes. The highest ranking one, Saeed Emami, mysteriously killed himself in jail before he could stand trial, but before his convenient suicide, apparently admitted not just to the murders but also to acting completely outside the authority of the government who employed him. As we all know, it's only ever a few bad apples.

Luckily, Emami apparently made a list before killing himself of all the murders he arranged, and the government apparently knew nothing about – and Farrokhzad's name wasn't on it. Now we can either believe Emami wrote the list, or we can believe the Iranian government did.

And if the Iranian government were using Emami to deflect – why miss such a high-profile name as Farrokhzad's off the list? If you're clearing house, why not blame the whole lot on a rogue element you've already made a scapegoat and clear the matter up once and for all?

Scene Ten

JAVAAD/NARRATOR (*as if he is writing the show*). I feel myself start to fail. I start to chip away at what's good about it, until I fuck it up again. Maybe I didn't know enough to start. Maybe that's it. I click another link, and another tab opens.

It's not about me, I think. It's about the effect and transformation I am trying to achieve for other people. And of course it's useful. It has to be. But once you start giving in to the way the building is tilting it falls again and again.

Once, a therapist asked me to tell him what kind of person I was. And all I could actually list was things I do. Retreating into something that felt like certainty when asked to fill an emptiness, where a part of me lived that resisted being seen.

So I square myself back up with what feels most real. I am taking all these facts and arranging them into a productive network that will change how people see themselves in the world. I'm doing it for them. Not for me. I'm not the one who feels like I'm drowning.

Scene Eleven

RAAM/MUSICIAN, *now properly live, speaking directly to the audience.*

RAAM/MUSICIAN. I don't know if it was Kambiz Hosseini or one of his team who chose to use 'The Hunter' over that footage, or how they found it. But that song made me a representation of something, in Persian, that I never meant to be. So people found the guy who wrote the song and told him things they couldn't say to anyone else.

'King Raam' – my recording name started as a kind of self-deprecating joke, but I guess I'm stuck with it – 'King Raam, we got home from the protest and we saw our friends beaten with metal bars and taken away, and we don't know where they are. Now we're sitting here drinking arak, and your song is the only thing that's helping, and we don't know what comes next. What comes next?' 'King Raam, I'm gay and I'm scared. What comes next?' 'King Raam. Who can I tell about the abuse I suffered when it was done by someone who also tells us sex is a shameful thing to talk about? What comes next?'

I try to answer them. I try to be helpful. I'm just a guy taking drugs in New York by this point, but it seems the least I can do. And for a few years, that's how it stays.

There's another election in Iran, and Hassan Rouhani gets in. The great reformist. We were all naively, briefly convinced that a real change was happening.

I go back to Iran, vaguely hopeful and, because of 'The Hunter', very fucking famous, and try to navigate the maze of state censorship. And Rouhani's promises of liberalisation turn to dust, as always, so I leave again.

And, soon after that the Revolutionary Guard arrest and torture my father on fictional spying charges, and two weeks later he dies in prison. By this time he was a trusted political analyst, a respected academic, and a fearless campaigner against environmental degradation. But ultimately it boiled down to: pissed off the wrong person in the wrong place at the wrong time. So they said he was a spy, discredited him, tortured him, and he died. He was the most humane and caring person I've ever met. And they killed him for it. That's it.

When my dad was killed, the regime ripped our family home apart, looking for evidence of something they knew they'd invented. So now, my mom wasn't just grieving but brutalised. Like us, she had the right to live in Canada. So we tried to get her out. She was put under house arrest. We had to leave our mother in the care of the regime that killed my father. There are worse things than his death.

I don't want you worrying about my mom for the rest of the show, so I'm going to tell you now – after a long fight, she lives in Canada these days with me. Or more accurately, I live in her basement, which is, I'm sure you'll agree, maximum rock 'n' roll. But this next bit of the story happens before we got her out.

I was in New York, I was in despair, I was in therapy. It didn't help. I was drinking a lot. It didn't help.

And Iran hadn't relaxed. In 2019 there was another uprising. More angry and radical than the last. About three thousand people were shot dead in the street in Tehran.

So I'm sitting in New York between their situation, and my mother's. And that was crushing me.

It came down to this. Kill myself, or do something else. So I did something else. One night, drunk, in my shitty apartment, I switched on a microphone, and I started talking about my life.

You heard me right. Like I said at the start, the Iranian regime has forced me to be Iranian. But in my darkest trauma, and my deepest despair, I found the most Western response possible. I started a fucking podcast.

I started talking about my life, and my dad, so he wouldn't be forgotten.

'Masty o Rasty' means 'The Drunken Truth' in Persian. It's from Ancient Greek maybe, I never really looked it up. But the idea is they'd solve a problem by talking it out, fucked out of their minds. Another word in Persian is 'taarof'. It's a whole system of etiquette as a kind of polite lying. I guess another title for what I accidentally did would be: 'Fuck Taarof, Let's Talk'.

And because I talked, people – young Iranian people – talked, openly, in a way that felt like they were getting the first opportunity to do it. And like 'The Hunter', it ran away into the distance and became its own thing. If I told you how many millions of people download the podcast these days, you'd think I was boasting, so I won't. But it's a lot.

So I guess that's what I do now. I talk and I listen to other people talk. People talking about the difference between the life they're forced to live and the one they want to live, and maybe inching closer to destroying the first in favour of the second.

And in the middle of it, me. Trying to work out how I got here and how not to cause disaster.

Scene Twelve

JAVAAD/NARRATOR. For two or three years, between around 2016 and 2018, a war raged on the Scots-language Wikipedia. Now for those who don't know, Scots is a language spoken in the lowlands of Scotland and Ulster. It's not Scottish Gaelic. Whether it is, so to speak, a proper language as opposed to a dialect of English is a matter of quite serious debate. It concerns not only education and cultural policy in Scotland, but – because it was spoken by the ancestors of some Northern Irish Protestants – the peace process in the north of Ireland. In that way, it's a matter of life and death.

In 2016 the front page of Scots language Wikipedia looked like this:

Projection.

As you can probably tell this isn't the Scots language that Robert Burns used, it's just English with a Hollywood Scottish accent.

That's because over the previous few years, an American teenager with a self-professed ignorance of Scots had written nearly two-thirds of the entries on Scots Wikipedia. Amaryllis Gardener, as they were known, admitted to knowing no Scots at all and basing their grasp of it mainly on their idea of what Scottish people sound like.

There were real-world consequences to this, not only in the sense that Amaryllis was banned from Wikipedia, but also in the real debates about how minority language rights should work in Scotland and Northern Ireland.

Amaryllis Gardner was faced with a gap in their knowledge of the world, and they decided to fill it with something that felt coherent and solid. Which in their case was a vague memory of watching *Braveheart*.

But we all do that, much more automatically, whenever we come across something we don't understand and try to put a framework together based on what we think we already know. It's how we think of the machines we have created to serve us facts, themselves. Of places like Wikipedia, because we don't think about who edits it, but actually of the whole internet. On some level, no matter how much we take the piss out of people who say this, we just do think of it as a series of boxes and tubes that no human is actually responsible for.

But the gods of the internet have fooled us. Look at Amazon. It doesn't make most of its money being the greatest grocer the world has ever known, but by providing internet services like cloud storage and data processing. And it does that by brokering cheap human labour.

We think that artificial intelligence is transforming our internet experience, tagging us in photos, training our Alexa, selecting adverts based on clicks. In fact, the vast vast majority of this data analysis is broken down into smaller jobs that can be carried out by the kind of lower-middle-class people in places that feel like the periphery, who have access to some sort of wifi and a laptop. For between seven and twenty-five cents an hour, they invisibly fill the gaps of the story we tell ourselves about what digital technology can do. A lot of the data we compulsively inject into our brains is from syringes prepared by real people in Costa Rica or Kyrgyzstan for pennies. We're used to thinking of colonialism as a past we can reverse the lingering damage of, but that's not how colonialism works. It's not even how the past works. It shapes the fabric of the modern world and its tools far more deeply than that. Like the ungoogleable history of the colonised and unrecorded, or the individuals who appear as an undifferentiated mass in our heads when I say the word 'refugees', the internet is invisible people, all the way down.

Amazon calls this hiring system 'Mechanical Turk', after the eighteenth-century humanoid machines – constructed so people would believe a machine could play chess, when in fact there was just a human player, hidden in a box below.

It's easy to laugh at Amaryllis Gardner, but there is an instinct we share with them. Resemblance. Representation. A sense of solid coherency. These are seductive things. Wanting the people, the experiences that exist in places we don't have access to to be knowable – making ourselves believe that knowledge is what's missing – it doesn't seem all that different to wanting Mel Gibson's accent in *Braveheart* to be the Scots language itself.

Scene Thirteen

Over the course of this podcast, ASHA/PODCASTER *feels like she is getting more and more lost in the layers of the mystery.*

ASHA/PODCASTER.Welcome to *Death in the Gaps.* A podcast that wants to shine a light on mysterious unsolved murders, revealing the truth behind the way the world works, and the invisible and deadly stories we don't even notice on our own bloodstained doorsteps. But you know this by now, and the more you know, the more you understand.

This series, we're looking at the mysterious murder of Fereydoun Farrokhzad. It's a mystery that is full of competing theories, and each episode, we've examined one of them. Each one of them is slightly more complicated and this one's no exception. Maybe it's the one that gets you closest. So focus, lean in, and let me connect the dots and fire the synapses. You wonder if 'synapses' is the right pronunciation and you reflexively google it. You wonder when 'google' was first recorded as a verb and you google it. July 8th, 1998, which seems pleasingly specific. Concrete. The more you know, the more you understand.

In the last two episodes we've looked at two theories – how it's unlikely Farrokhzad was killed by someone he knew well, and how it's unlikely he was killed directly by the Iranian secret police. But if neither of these stories are true – what if both of them are?

We need to fill the void with facts again. And relearn the context, so we can understand those facts. The more you know, the more you understand.

First, we know that at least one person was in Farrokhzad's apartment with him – and we know that Farrokhzad was probably making dinner for them both. You imagine an Iranian dinner – strong sense of pomegranate – and you remember some controversy about Persian-style hummus that this is moving too fast for you to look up right now. If you were to explain a pomegranate, you might say it's like an apple, in the same way Farrokhzad is like Tom Jones. Same basic shape but somehow multitudes inside it.

So the murderer was someone he was expecting, and someone who he presumably didn't suspect would harm him. But we also know it was someone aware enough to take incriminating evidence, like Farrokhzad's camera and planner, away. Let's call this emerging suspect Mr X – this is a murder-mystery podcast after all, and Mr X sounds suitably mysterious.

In 2019, a transcript of an interview with Abolghasem Mesbahi was leaked to *Voice of America*'s Persian-language station. Mesbahi was a former spy who defected to Germany in the mid-1990s. He helped to convict four of Iran's agents who had been involved in killing dissidents overseas. He's obviously a man who knows things. You're not sure you knew that *Voice of America* had a Persian-language station. And you find, as you take your iPhone out of your pocket – it's a continuation of the Cold War *Voice of America* that used to broadcast US-branded freedom into countries that didn't yet have the benefit. That's pretty weird, why should you trust *Voice of America*? You decide to take me at my word.

Mesbahi claimed to have information on the Farrokhzad case. He says Mr X was a friend of Farrokhzad's based in Los Angeles, who contacted Iranian intelligence through intermediaries. He was able to kill Fereydoun because he was already very close to him. He could go into his home without being suspected. Mesbahi said that Mr X was a royalist, who wanted to reclaim assets that had been confiscated by the Iranian regime following the 1979 revolution. And even though Khomeini had deposed the Royal Family, and taken the assets of the elite class associated with them, in certain, very exceptional circumstances, there seems to have been a way back from this.

Apparently, anyone that wanted to return to Iran and get their property back had to prove their renewed loyalty to the state – a process that could, and occasionally did, involve committing murder on its behalf.

Farrokhzad himself wasn't necessarily a royalist, as such, but by this stage, your enemy's enemy was your friend. And if that was cemented by a picture of the Shah, so be it.

Through the mid-1980s, Fereydoun lived on and off in LA. So did Mr X. Farrokhzad often appeared on LA-based, Persian-language television programmes. Two producers remember Mr X visiting their local studios with the exiled singer.

Now it might sound weird that two Iranian exiles could meet at a Persian-language TV station in LA, so you need to know what LA means in Iranian culture – people call it Tehran-geles because it's got so many Iranians. You google how many Iranians live in southern California and there are like nearly a million. The more you know, the more you understand. But it's complicated. A small and important minority of them are the people who used to run the country, and fled with millions of dollars, and the vast majority are just immigrants trying to live the American Dream. So LA isn't just LA like we would think of it.

So it's unsurprising in a way Farrokhzad would find himself there. On and off throughout the eighties. But he'd returned to Germany in 1989. Maybe he was hoping to return to Iran like the many exiles who were being let back in at this time. Maybe Germany just felt closer, more friendly to that aspiration. A step towards an eventual reconciliation.

I guess this tells us something about his state of mind in the run-up to his death. Tom Jones is always going to miss the 'Green Green Grass of Home' and exiled Farrokhzad, in front of thousands of adoring fans, berating the government that will eventually kill him, will always still miss Tehran.

We're not sure if Farrokhzad wanted to go back to Iran. We do know that he was isolated and probably less sharp and critical at working out who his friends were.

And we don't know much about Mr X really, this false friend and alleged killer, except that he lived in LA, or the version of LA where elite Iranians in exile lived. And that he, too, probably wanted to go home.

So this is what happened.

Mr X would have lived in the West, probably LA, since the revolution. He would have dreamed of going home and taking power again, but that would be obviously off the cards now. Maybe the money he had spirited out of the country was running out.

According to Mesbahi, in Iran, Mr X could have received specialist training, from someone like Saeed Emami who orchestrated the chain killings. He would be told not to take any weapons, because if they were later found they could give investigators a lead. He would know not to be seen, and to ask Farrokhzad not to meet him at the train station.

You think about wanting two different things at the same time. To want to be in a country and to hate it, from outside it. To love a singer and to want to bring to power a government that will have him killed. To look at a friend and see killing him as the only way to get a semblance of your former life back. To love something and be sick of it.

He would have been trained to use something in the house to kill Fereydoun. Like a kitchen knife, for example, and to make sure that the first blow was in the neck, as that would silence him. He would know about Fereydoun's habit of taking memento photos of his visitors, and the planner he kept his diary in. He would know to go straight to the airport and get back on a plane to Iran. He would know that, having shown his loyalty, he would get his land and his passport back, and never be found.

So in a way, both of these things are true. Farrokhzad was killed for deeply personal reasons, by an individual he knew. And he was killed by the state, using that individual as a weapon, because he was a structural inconvenience. A live wire that needed the current permanently switched off before it caused more damage.

None of this is certain, but of all the uncertainty, this is the chain of possible events that feels strongest.

Obviously, I know that there are loads of things there that it's hard to get your head around. What things meant in the context of the time. But that's how Fereydoun Farrokhzad was killed. The more you know, the more you understand.

As ever, please like and subscribe. Follow us on Twitter and Instagram on @ditgaps. We are available on iTunes, Spotify, and almost anywhere else you download quality podcasts.

Scene Fourteen

RAAM/MUSICIAN (*directly to audience*). So now I live in Vancouver. In my mom's basement. Which is useful to remind millions of podcast listeners, if they start thinking I'm a big deal.

And one summer day, not long ago, there's a knock on the door. I'm not in the basement, I'm in the backyard, barbecuing with no shirt on, because I'm Canadian now.

Who's at the door? You're wondering. Is it some romantic and uplifting conclusion to this story?

No, it's the Canadian Secret Service. Who sadly don't have black Mountie uniforms or arrive on horseback. They look ordinary, which I guess is the point. One of them's a brown guy like me, which is surprising. He also claims to be called Steve, which is implausible.

Apparently they got some information from the FBI. Okay I'm with you. There's an Iranian journalist in New York, Masih Alinejad, who's very public about women's rights and organises protests against the government's modesty codes. Right, guys, I'm aware of her already, in fact I'm in awe of her courage. The Iranian government have sent two people with instructions to kill her. Depressing and concerning, but not surprising. When they were intercepted, one of them had a list of names. Interesting. They were names of people the Iranian government would like to kill. That doesn't sound ideal. Your name was on it. Oh, fuck.

So I'm thinking, this is where you guys bundle me and my mom into a helicopter and take us to the super-secure facility up north for our own protection until danger passes.

Come on. This is Canada. What I get is, there's probably no need to worry, eh? But take precautions, and maybe don't go to any of the countries bordering Iran, because people get kidnapped there and we'd find it very difficult to help you. Eh? Also maybe don't tell anyone we were here. And probably don't talk about it in public. Eh? But as you've probably worked out by now, I'm not the best at taking advice.

So over the next couple of years, I find myself in a new space. Invited by human rights groups to share my story. I meet Uighur and Nigerian and Saudi Arabian dissidents that are going through the same thing. And when I'm asked about what living under that kind of threat feels like I try and explain. I can translate one of those worlds to the other. But I can't take you there, and I can't bring them here. It's beyond explaining the facts – it's a different kind of understanding. Like how I'm a rock star and a waiter in an upscale kebab shop. And both of those things are true.

And when, just recently, a young Kurdish-Iranian woman, Mahsa Amini, is beaten to death for not keeping to the proper hijab codes, and Iranian women explode into the most radical anti-regime movement in our history, I get swept up in that. Iranians use my podcast as a platform, sharing information on police tactics and calls for help and solidarity.

For whatever reason I've come to stand for something. Actually different things, for Iranians and for people internationally who want to help. For reasons I didn't intend. But for reasons I stand by. Not because of anything special I do or think. But because I've accidentally allowed other people to talk openly about the things they do and think.

And I think that's because I've been accidentally asking the question my father was asking all his life too. The question that regimes that rely on control and fear and violence can't support. Because when it's asked of them, they don't have a good answer to it.

Why does this thing happen, in this way?

It's a question it's easy for an artist to ask, but impossible for oppressive regimes to engage with – because it admits the possibility of being wrong, and apology, and change.

And I'm going to keep asking it. I guess until things change or they shoot me.

By the way, if there's anyone in the audience who was planning to shoot me tonight, now would be the most artistically useful moment to do it. No? Maybe tomorrow, then.

I'm not comparing myself to my dad, or to Neda Agha-Soltan or the hundreds of thousands of young women and men right now fighting for justice, freedom and a woman's right to choose her own path. To anyone who's a better human than me, and has paid a higher price than I hope I'll ever pay. I'm not comparing myself to Farrokhzad.

I'm like him. I'm not like him. I'm definitely not like Tom Jones. I can say all those things with confidence. But the one thing I'll never say, is that I understand the reasons behind any of it.

Beat.

Scene Fifteen

This final podcast has ASHA/PODCASTER *come completely unmoored from reality. [In the original production this was done by mixing live and recorded versions of the podcast: a pre-recording of* ASHA *gave the speech, whilst the real* ASHA *tried to make a huge visual representation of the murder in her podcast studio.]*

ASHA/PODCASTER. Welcome to our bonus episode. Patreon-only content. The real deep-dive that knits it all together.

This is about the context of what we've learned. Learning how it fits in with what we already know.

Chop an onion. Do the washing up. I walk you through the links. A different world. (*Mispronouncing*.) Synapsis – (*Correcting herself*.) synapses pronunciation doesn't matter. In your kitchen. Imagine tabs. Revolutions. Two dogs barking. Tectonic movements of history. Human blood and fat congealed. In his kitchen. Traditional Iranian nougat. Pomegranates.

A pomegranate is basically an apple. Farrokhzad is basically Tom Jones. Same basic shape, multitudes inside it.

Everything is like everything else.

The Iranian revolution? Wikipedia, scroll down third hyperlink. Khomeini and Iranians are Shia Muslims. Click blue text. There are eleven dead Imams in the Iranian branch of Shia Islam, and the twelfth is a messiah, who will return. Islam is like Judaism, Farrokhzad is like Tom Jones. Pomegranates are like apples.

New tab. More hot water and soap.

Social change in the Iranian revolution? Property seizure. Property reform. *The Protestant Ethic and the Spirit of Capitalism*. Like the Swiss Protestant reformation.

Google Translate Mesbahi, you'll get the literal translation 'my lamp'. But that's Arabic not Persian. This is like you've googled the French etymology of an English person's name, but you are not English and thinking about it in Dutch. And if Khomeini is a Jewish cleric going through a Protestant reformation. Apples are like pomegranates.

Tab five, *Voice of America* on Wikipedia. There are fifty countries where *Voice of America* broadcasts. They don't have freedom of the press. Iran is like all of them in that they are only like themselves.

The Iranian diaspora. Diasporic politics. People who leave are, maybe, like each other. Two thousand Sudanese in Helsinki are like ten thousand Bangladeshis in Manchester or eighty thousand Venezuelans in Madrid or a million Iranians in Los Angeles. But not a million Belgians in Cardiff, who don't exist, because the world didn't make them happen.

Those Iranians in Los Angeles are both like and not like themselves. And Los Angeles to them is different to what it is to us. The easiest way to understand them and that is to think Cuba is Iran and Batista is the Shah. In that sense Tehran-geles is like Miami. Cuba is also a Third World country. But at least they speak Spanish. You've been to Spain. They don't speak Persian. There is *Scarface*. Al Pacino is Cuban. No. That's Andy Garcia.

Just, imagine you are not hearing me say this in English. I am speaking in Persian. Which you understand because you watched *Braveheart* and Mel Gibson taught you Persian. You know exactly what *Voice of America* is but you know it in Persian.

The sort of Shia Jewish clergy of Iran, then, have radicalised into an early modern, modernising, Swiss Protestant radicalism, so some people have lost everything. Some people have gained everything. A man who is called 'My Lamp' in French, which you recognise because you speak French, but in English, which you don't, because your Dutch, tells you, on *Voice of America*, in Scottish-Persian, that an effect of this is that there are royalists who want to come back to the country, and that they can if they pay the price.

So, Tom Jones who has been driven from Switzerland into Bonn, which is neither Wales nor Las Vegas, becomes nothing more than a gap, in a story that someone needs to cross. Mr X, who is in Miami, and needs to get back to Cuba, if *Scarface*-Cuba was Iran and *Scarface* was set in Cuba. And Khomeini, who is Castro is saying he can come back, except Khomeini is like that girl from *Peanuts*, google it, Lucy, who always held the football and persuaded Charlie Brown to kick it then pulled it away at the last second, if pulling the football away at the last second was the same as getting another exile to brutally murder you while your back was turned and if Charlie Brown's humiliation after falling for the trick, the same trick every fucking time, was like the silence of a voice that used to have the most popular variety show on Iranian TV before Lucy, who is like Khomeini, who is the Castro to the Shah's Batista, pulled away the football, which is your life. It's complicated. But the more you know, the more you understand.

You scratch repeatedly at a stain on a plate. You can't hear the podcast over running water.

Under the water the information keeps flowing, and you can dip your hands into it whenever you like. Dipping your hands in it is like fooling yourself you know water when all you can catch are the things it carries. Twigs and bright fish. You wonder what the biggest river in Iran is and think how strange it feels that Iran might have big rivers. You wonder how we can ever really know if anything really happens or why. Things happen and the reasons for them are unrecorded, because how would such a thing even be possible, and we fool ourselves they were inevitable by picking up the pieces, or at least things that look most like pieces afterwards and making them into a construction and we say if this construction is the frame we all share, then it must make sense of this, of two versions of the same person speaking about making sense, seen from as many fractionally different perspectives as there are minds in a room, unsure if the past is responding to the present, or the present the past. It must make sense of everyone, everywhere, and everything, and anything unseen is unimportant and that is like Farrokhzad, who is like a pomegranate who is like Tom Jones because everything must be like something we know or we may have to accept the world we thought was the world is not like that at all.

The more you know, the more you... know.

Scene Sixteen

JAVAAD/NARRATOR (*as if he is writing the play*). So I square myself back up with what feels most real.

There is a feeling of chattering voices. Their poly-vocal reverberation on the inside of my skin and the edges of my bones. The description makes them fact, the fact fills the void. I still need to do it. Even though it doesn't seem to help.

If you're not sure of who you are, you can at least be sure of what you know.

This is just the structure I reach out for, to keep myself from falling into the great black hole at the centre of my engagement in the world. That sense of overload. Inertia. Stood still. Cut off. It's something that I see all around me. Live feed news updates of a news conference where you know what will be said. What you think causes market crashes, the sudden movement of people or the decisions that govern whether strangers live or die. Sitting in darkness trying to explain the murder of a cultural icon who is fundamental to one half of you, and invisible to the other. Sitting in a theatre, listening to a disembodied voice, speaking facts into a different kind of darkness, maybe mistaking the feeling of knowing about the world for being able to change it.

Scene Seventeen

As JAVAAD/NARRATOR *finishes speaking, a shift in light and projection causes the podcast studio to melt away.*
ASHA/PODCASTER *and* JAVAAD/NARRATOR *are stood in Fereydoun Farrokhzad's flat at the moment of the murder.*

They try and describe what is happening.

ASHA/PODCASTER. To put it another way. At the end of his life Fereydoun Farrokhzad fell through the subaltern gaps of the Global North where refugees live and dissidents can be killed.

We only know some basic facts. This flat above a grocer's shop. This small galley kitchen opening on this small main room, two dogs in that separate bedroom. A fifth-generation tape recording of Iranian popular music. Total floor space of around thirty-five square metres. To fill anything else in is conjecture.

JAVAAD/NARRATOR. If we believe the Mr X theory, he would have had to find a moment in the kitchen, when Fereydoun's back was turned.

ASHA/PODCASTER. Fereydoun says, maybe, people like us are cursed to love a country that might never have us back.

JAVAAD/NARRATOR. The guest wants to agree, but his voice catches in his throat.

ASHA/PODCASTER. Farrokhzad feels alive.

JAVAAD/NARRATOR. The frame of anger, of righteous fucking anger at the world taken from him gives shape to the things that feel increasingly necessary to say.

ASHA/PODCASTER. He tells his guest; he has fewer and fewer friends left. They keep telling him Khomeini wants him dead.

JAVAAD/NARRATOR. 'He's not the only one' he says.

ASHA/PODCASTER. He's marked for death just for telling what he considers to be the truth.

JAVAAD/NARRATOR. Fereydoun would have to have been hit from behind.

ASHA/PODCASTER. Roughly here, the body had to fall in such a way that when it was discovered, the bowls of fruit, nuts and nougat had been knocked over –

JAVAAD/NARRATOR. – but close enough to the open oven door, for his skin to have been burned, and blood and fat to have been congealed.

ASHA/PODCASTER. Fereydoun opens the oven door. His guest comes into the kitchen. Fereydoun insists he sit back down to be served; his guest tells him they're too close to stand on formalities.

JAVAAD/NARRATOR. According to what we have seen of the German police transcript, Fereydoun would have been stabbed around a dozen times with differing levels of force. He would have been dead by the fifth blow.

ASHA/PODCASTER. Probably in that moment – Fereydoun is just really tightly focused on making the cheap gas oven ignite.

JAVAAD/NARRATOR. Tunnel vision –

ASHA/PODCASTER. – click –

JAVAAD/NARRATOR. – click –

ASHA/PODCASTER. – flame.

JAVAAD/NARRATOR. Strike.

ASHA/PODCASTER. The brute force of the pain, from nothing, fills Fereydoun's mind.

JAVAAD/NARRATOR. Strike.

ASHA/PODCASTER. His hands go up instinctively, he tries to grasp against something as his head is pulled back.

JAVAAD/NARRATOR. He can't see what is happening.

ASHA/PODCASTER. Strike.

JAVAAD/NARRATOR. The music from the tape and the kitchen and the oven, the floor.

ASHA/PODCASTER. Everything is closing in and the pain is like a brilliant white and everything folds inwards.

JAVAAD/NARRATOR. Strike.

ASHA/PODCASTER. Fereydoun slips in and out of consciousness.

JAVAAD/NARRATOR. He sees himself from outside.

ASHA/PODCASTER. Hours pass.

JAVAAD/NARRATOR. Blank.

ASHA/PODCASTER. Half a heartbeat passes.

JAVAAD/NARRATOR. Inside his eyes again.

ASHA/PODCASTER. Slow realisation of who is doing what to him.

JAVAAD/NARRATOR. Connections between betrayal.

ASHA/PODCASTER. Pain.

JAVAAD/NARRATOR. Strike.

ASHA/PODCASTER. Maybe he knew more as he left the world than when he came into it.

JAVAAD/NARRATOR. It feels like we know more about why he died, now.

ASHA/PODCASTER. But we don't.

JAVAAD/NARRATOR. Not really.

ASHA/PODCASTER. There was a singer.

JAVAAD/NARRATOR. There was a poet.

ASHA/PODCASTER. There was a revolution.

JAVAAD/NARRATOR. There was a refugee.

ASHA/PODCASTER. There were speeches.

JAVAAD/NARRATOR. There were concerts.

ASHA/PODCASTER. There was an apartment, above a small shop.

JAVAAD/NARRATOR. There was fame.

ASHA/PODCASTER. There was an invisible foreigner.

JAVAAD/NARRATOR. There were competing ideas about who got to speak for a country, and about love, and God.

ASHA/PODCASTER. There was a life, and then there wasn't.

JAVAAD/NARRATOR. Silence is like nothing, except silence.

Scene Eighteen

JAVAAD/NARRATOR. About an hour and a half ago, I threatened to do a version of this show that centred my identity, and was about my place in a diaspora. A show about the truth of being made by two worlds.

That would have ended differently. I'd step down to meet you all and pass out examples of the traditional Iranian nougat that is referenced throughout the show, as a taste – a direct experience of difference that cuts through all the political complications we live with and makes a feeling of a world outside this room alive, in your mouth. And as we tasted that nougat, we'd know more, and we'd understand.

And at the heart of that would be the absolute and seductive lie that says: when something feels completely other to us, we can get a sort of direct experience of it, like the taste and texture of a kind of nougat.

It says that everything, in principle, can be known. That we all share a universal set of intellectual tools, a universal set of machines. And we can plug anyone's experience or history into them, and enhance our network of understanding.

But different truths live within and around each other, with different levels of power and visibility.

Farrokhzad in a grocer's in Bonn. Another Iranian refugee sees Tom Jones buying an aubergine. A white German sees one brown refugee look at another, stunned, as he haggles over vegetable pricing.

Both things are true. They were true then, and they're true now.

Somewhere in this city, there's a displaced Pakistani journalist. There's a former student from Hong Kong in Sydney, an Eritrean poet in Philadelphia. In a city we've never heard of, there's the King Raam or Fereydoun Farrokhzad of a country we haven't even mentioned. We can choose to try and live as if we are aware of them or we can choose not to. They don't choose. That's the void between us and them.

And in that same way, there is a void beyond that, which from our side we can only see the edges of, where the kinds of people doing jobs for 'Mechanical Turk' live. And beyond that, people just dreaming of even affording a laptop to do that kind of job in a slum in Asmara or Karachi, or Tehran. Dancing to pop stars we've never heard of, invisible to history themselves, but making history, all the time.

And should one of their grandchildren, in an unlikely turn of events, end up making theatre in this visible world, he won't even be able to see them either. You can't just read them off against your own understanding of how the world is supposed to work, like you're popping a piece of nougat in your mouth.

The tools we use trick us into thinking our fragmented world can be drawn together. But it can't. We can't make the invisible visible in that way. But we can choose to recognise it's out there.

You can't do that with nougat. I'm not sure the nougat even exists.

Because nothing is really like anything else, not in that way. Not in a way that will help us or the Fereydoun Farrokhzads of today. If that way of understanding could really make a difference – there would be a place on this planet where I'd be able to explain Tom Jones by telling whoever was sitting where you are now, he's a bit like the Welsh Fereydoun Farrokhzad. And there isn't.

A Nick Hern Book

Things Hidden Since the Foundation of the World first published in Great Britain in 2023 as a paperback original by Nick Hern Books Limited, The Glasshouse, 49a Goldhawk Road, London W12 8QP, in association with The Javaad Alipoor Company

Things Hidden Since the Foundation of the World copyright © 2023 Javaad Alipoor, Chris Thorpe

Javaad Alipoor and Chris Thorpe have asserted their right to be identified as the authors of this work

Cover image © photography: Chris Payne; design: Adam York Gregory

Designed and typeset by Nick Hern Books, London
Printed in Great Britain by Mimeo Ltd, Huntingdon, Cambridgeshire PE29 6XX

A CIP catalogue record for this book is available from the British Library

ISBN 978 1 83904 273 7

www.nickhernbooks.co.uk/environmental-policy

www.nickhernbooks.co.uk

facebook.com/nickhernbooks

twitter.com/nickhernbooks